W9-BCT-077

BIG IDEAS in SCIENCE

THE THEORY OF
RELATIVITY

Katie Parker

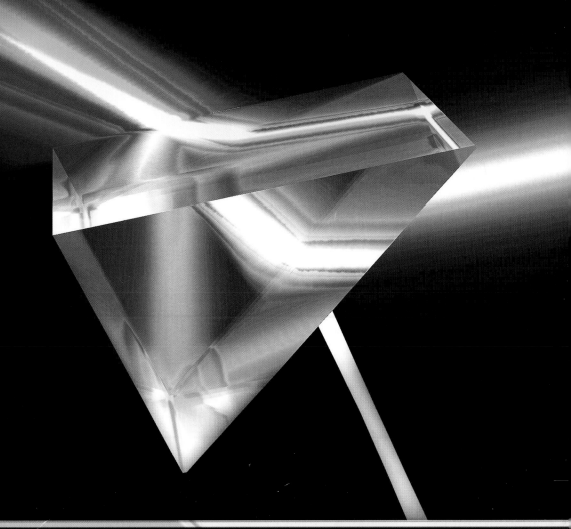

This edition first published in 2010 in the United States
of America by Marshall Cavendish Benchmark.

Marshall Cavendish Benchmark
99 White Plains Road
Tarrytown, NY 10591
www.marshallcavendish.us

Library of Congress Cataloging-in-Publication Data
Parker, Katie, 1974–
The theory of relativity / by Katie Parker.
p. cm.—(Big ideas in science)
Summary: "Provides comprehensive information on the theory of relativity
and how it affects our lives today"—Provided by publisher.
Includes bibliographical references and index.
ISBN 978-0-7614-4398-8
1. Relativity (Physics)—Juvenile literature. I. Title.
QC173.575.P367 2010
530.11—dc22
2008055991

530.11
PAR

The photographs in this book are used by permission and through the courtesy of:
Cover: NASA; Dreamstime
Half Title: Shutterstock
P4tl: J. McPhail/Shutterstock; P4br: Péter Gudella/Shutterstock; P5: Peter Titmuss/Alamy;
P7: Andreas Ehrhard/Alamy; P8: Adam Woolfitt/Photolibrary; P9: Gustavo Tomsich/Corbis;
P11: Richard Hamill/Shutterstock; P12: mary evan picture library/Photolibrary;
P13: Photolibrary; P17: Kevin Fleming/Corbis; P19: Shutterstock; Pp20-21: Fotolia;
P21(inset): Galdzer/Dreamstime; P22: The Gallery Collection/Corbis; P23: Rudy Sulgan/
Corbis; P26: Bettman/Corbis; Pp28-29: Roger Ressmeyer/Corbis; P30: NASA;
P30bg: Roger Ressmeyer/Corbis; P31bl: Anatoliy Babiychuk/Shutterstock;
P31br: Fotobacca/Shutterstock; P32: CERN; P33: CERN; P34: Bettmann/Corbis;
P37: NASA; P38: National Institute of Standards and Technology; P39: Photolibrary;
P40: NASA; Pp42-43: Shutterstock; P43(inset): Raguet/Phanie/Rex Features; P45: NASA.
Illustrations: Q2AMedia Art Bank

Created by Q2AMedia
Art Director: Sumit Charles
Editor: Denise Pangia
Series Editor: Penny Dowdy
Client Service Manager: Santosh Vasudevan
Project Manager: Shekhar Kapur
Designer: Shilpi Sarkar and Joita Das
Illustrators: Prachand Verma, Ajay Sharma,
Bibin Jose, Abhideep Jha and Rajesh Das
Photo Research: Shreya Sharma

Printed in Malaysia

135642

Contents

It's All Relative 4

Motion 6

Time 10

Space 14

Light 18

Newtonian Physics 22

Einstein Connects the Pieces: The Special
Theory of Relativity 26

Special Thought Experiments and Proofs 30

The General Theory of Relativity 34

General Thought Experiments and Proofs 38

What's Relativity Got to Do with It? 42

Glossary 46

Find Out More 47

Index 48

This boy feels as if he is standing on solid ground, and not moving at all. Do you think that's true?

It's All Relative

Have you ever heard the expression, "Everything is relative"? It means that there may be more than one way of looking at a situation. Now physicists have given us proof that many things really are relative!

Here's an example of a situation that can be viewed in more than one way. The boy looking at the train sees only a blur as it speeds by. He feels as though he is not moving at all.

Now look at the picture of the girl in the train. When she looks out the window, she sees the world flying by. Like the boy, she feels as though she isn't moving at all. Her soda doesn't even spill!

So who is right, the boy or the girl? According to modern physics, they both are. It's all relative!

4

This girl thinks the world outside is flying by, and that she is sitting still.

Here is another situation that can be viewed in more than one way: a man looking down on New York City from a plane might think the buildings are tiny. A woman on the ground looking up at the buildings might think the exact opposite. Yet, they're both right! They see things differently because they are looking from a different frame of reference, or specific position and speed.

Albert Einstein had two theories about relativity: the General Theory and the Special Theory. You just learned the basis of the Special Theory. Einstein's theories are more complicated than the examples you just read. They involve physics, which is the study of matter and energy, and astronomy, which is the study of matter in outer **space**. You've just learned from the examples that relativity depends on a different frame of reference. You are about to find out that these small examples can be expanded into larger situations, which involve the entire universe. Just about everything in the universe is relative.

Einstein was a genius, but with a little background on motion, time, space, and light, anyone can understand his relativity theories. Then, you can connect them just like Einstein did. You may even begin to see things differently, too!

When you hear a car horn, does it sound like the noise is getting lower immediately after the car passes by? This perception has a scientific basis, which is called the Doppler Effect, named after Christian Doppler, who discovered it. Sound moves in waves. Its **pitch** depends on the **wavelength** and **frequency** of the waves. When a source of sound moves, these properties change, too. They also change if an observer moves. If you rode your bike past a ringing pay phone, the ringing would sound lower once you passed it. Like sound, relative observations about motion, time, and space also have a scientific basis.

Motion

If you're wondering about space and time, you could be the next Albert Einstein! Space and time consumed him, as it did many great minds over the centuries. Ancient civilizations admitted that they could not completely understand nature's mysteries. Yet, that didn't stop them from trying!

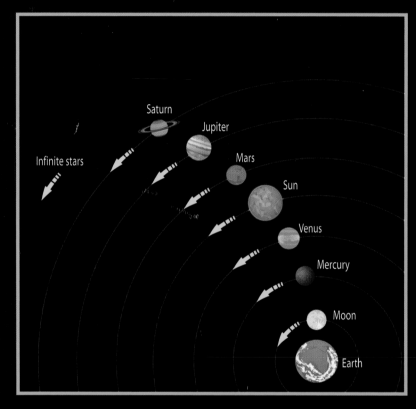

In a geocentric model like this one, each of the planets and stars are part of their own crystal sphere. All of the spheres circled Earth, the center of the universe.

Imagine what it was like for people living in ancient times. Looking into the sky, they could see the stars and the Sun floating in space, and they were left with questions: How do objects float in space? Why does the Sun rise and set each day? Most importantly, how is our planet related to the rest of the universe?

Ancient Greeks noticed that the planets seemed to move, but the stars did not. Ptolemy, a famous astronomer, formulated a geocentric, or Earth-centered, model to explain the motion of the universe. In his model, Earth was at the center of the solar system. The Sun, Moon, and known planets circled around Earth. This pleased the Greeks, who felt that the universe was an orderly place. It was also nice to believe that our planet and we humans were special. After all, we were at the center of everything.

The geocentric model, which was popular for over 1,400 years, showed that Earth was surrounded by many crystal spheres, each holding a planet or stars. The spheres that held stars were fixed in place, so stars did not move. Those that held planets circled around Earth.

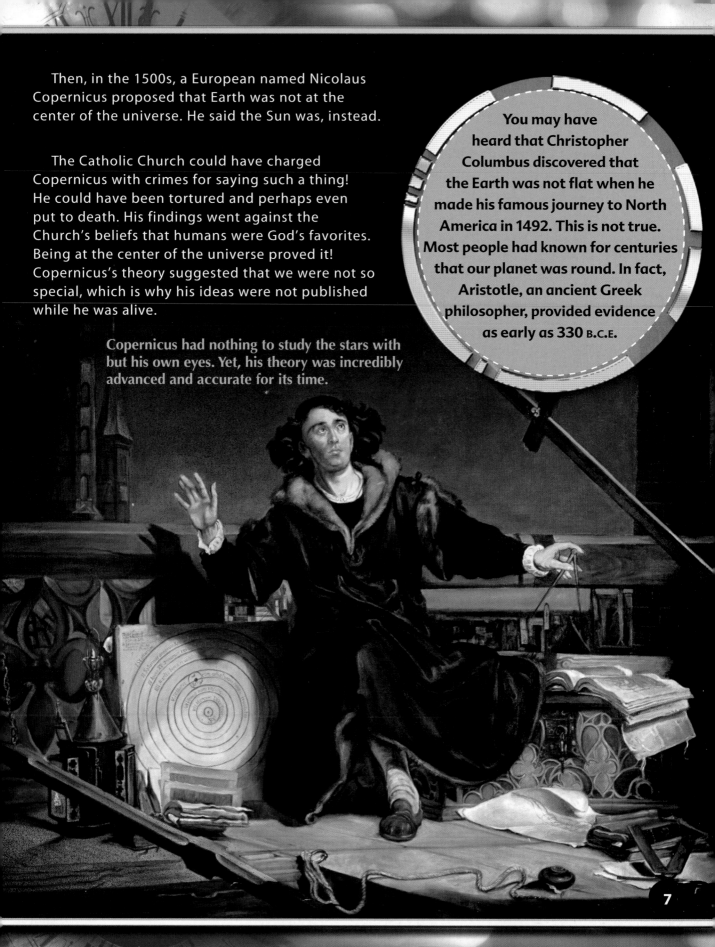

Then, in the 1500s, a European named Nicolaus Copernicus proposed that Earth was not at the center of the universe. He said the Sun was, instead.

The Catholic Church could have charged Copernicus with crimes for saying such a thing! He could have been tortured and perhaps even put to death. His findings went against the Church's beliefs that humans were God's favorites. Being at the center of the universe proved it! Copernicus's theory suggested that we were not so special, which is why his ideas were not published while he was alive.

You may have heard that Christopher Columbus discovered that the Earth was not flat when he made his famous journey to North America in 1492. This is not true. Most people had known for centuries that our planet was round. In fact, Aristotle, an ancient Greek philosopher, provided evidence as early as 330 B.C.E.

Copernicus had nothing to study the stars with but his own eyes. Yet, his theory was incredibly advanced and accurate for its time.

The findings of Copernicus were published in Latin after his death. Only scholars could read the language. Most of them were afraid of the Church's reaction, but some found Copernicus's writing enlightening and went on to read it anyway. The Catholic Church controlled the government and the universities. If Church leaders did not agree with information that was taught or published, they could arrest the scholar and put him in jail.

Galileo Galilei was an Italian mathematician. He agreed with Copernicus about a heliocentric model, which is a model of the universe where the Sun is at the center. Galileo was the first known astronomer to study the heavens with a tool that improved the ability to see space. This tool was the telescope. He could see that the planets, including Earth, orbit, or circle, the Sun.

In 1610 Galileo published a book called *Starry Messenger*. He wrote about what he saw when he turned his telescope to the heavens, which was that many stars that appear small are just farther away than we thought. He watched four **bodies** that circled Jupiter. He noticed that their positions changed from night to night. He realized that Jupiter must have four moons! He also wrote about his **lunar** observations. He noted that the Moon was not smooth and perfectly round. It had craters and mountains.

Many ancient civilizations developed tools to help them study the world. This instrument, an astrolabe, helped sailors navigate their way. Long before Copernicus and Galileo, this tool could predict the position of stars and planets—based on a heliocentric model.

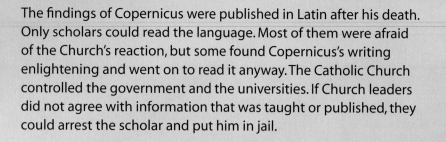

Galileo did not escape controversy. Much as the Catholic Church took issue with Copernicus, so it had problems with Galileo. Galileo had to state that both he and Copernicus were wrong. He also had to spend the last eight years of his life under house arrest.

Now, the world acknowledges Galileo's gifts to science. He gave proof of how Earth and the planets move in space. The telescope opened up a new world of possibilities for studying space and time. Galileo's findings are the basis for modern astronomy.

Galileo was the first astronomer to study the skies with a telescope. Once he did, he had all the proof he needed that Copernicus was right about the Sun being the center of the universe.

Galileo is often credited with inventing the telescope, but actually he didn't. In fact, in 1608, a Dutch astronomer named Hans Lipperhey applied for a patent, or right of ownership. Even newer evidence shows that the true inventor may have been Juan Roget, a spectacle-maker living in Spain. A book written in 1609 by an Italian named Girolamo Sirtori called Roget the real inventor. Death records from Roget's time cataloged goods owned by those who died. One, from 1593, was described as a long eyeglass decorated with brass.

Time

Figuring out how Earth moved in space was a big accomplishment. This knowledge could be used to answer more questions about time, space, and movement. King Charles II opened an observatory in Greenwich, England, to study astronomy. He hoped to research an accurate system of measuring the Earth's distances to help sailors navigate the seas.

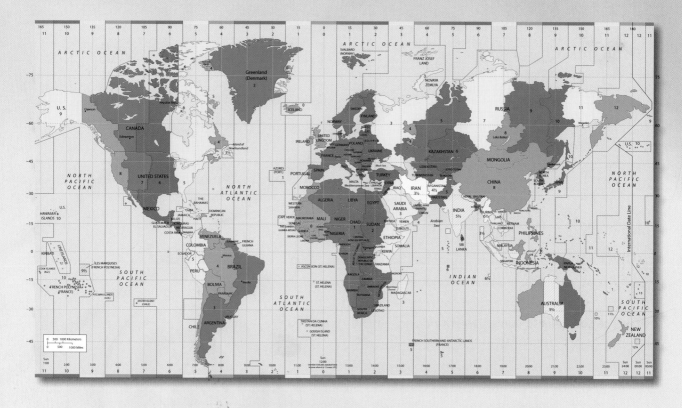

The time zone in England is called Greenwich Mean Time (GMT). A city that is eight time zones west of GMT would be eight hours earlier, and a city that is eight zones east would be eight hours later. When you are leaving school for the day, a student in England might be going to sleep.

At the Royal Greenwich **Observatory**, astronomers discovered that they could measure time very precisely based on Earth's movement through space. It takes twenty-four hours for Earth to rotate. Earth has twenty-four **time zones**, 15 degrees apart, running between the North and South poles. Each line of **longitude** represents a different time zone.

The Prime Meridian is the longitude line that runs through Greenwich, England, at 0 degrees, 0 minutes, 0 seconds. Every new day and year starts here. All other time zones are measured in their relation to the Prime Meridian. Each time zone is an hour earlier than the time zone to the east of it. In other words, the correct time depends on your position on Earth. Even time is relative!

In 1884 a Canadian citizen named Sir Sanford Fleming helped organize a conference in Washington, D.C., which was held to standardize time. Until then, countries, states, and cities often used their own local time, resulting in mass confusion. Fleming is known as the Father of Standardized Time. Frustration was his inspiration. He missed a train in Ireland because of confusion over time. Yet, Fleming also was inspired by other inventions. He actually designed an early version of inline skates, which are a type of roller skate!

It's hard to think of time as a concept separate from timekeeping. We measure time in seconds, minutes, and hours. Days, weeks, months, and years pass. Remember, people made this system of timekeeping because it is convenient for us. So why did we decide to put sixty minutes in an hour? Earth is round, and there are 360 degrees in a sphere. It is no coincidence that 360 divided by 15 is exactly 24, or the number of hours in a day. That means Earth takes one hour, or sixty minutes, to rotate 15 degrees.

Suppose that astronomers at the Royal Observatory placed longitude lines every 10 degrees. We would have thirty-six hours in a day. Yet, to correspond to the natural events such as the sunrise and sunset, the hours would be shorter: about forty minutes.

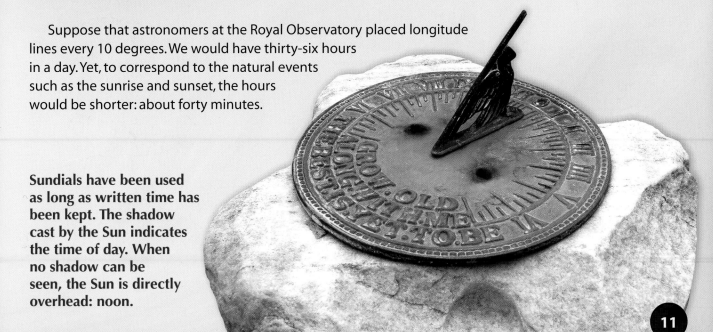

Sundials have been used as long as written time has been kept. The shadow cast by the Sun indicates the time of day. When no shadow can be seen, the Sun is directly overhead: noon.

Even ancient cultures divided the days into twenty-four hours. In addition, they did it without any knowledge of how the Earth moved. Their techniques were based only on their observations of the sky. For them, both day and night were twelve hours long. Ancient Greeks and Romans simply had longer daylight hours during the summer, while in the winter, each hour was shorter because there was less daylight.

Archaeologists found a **sundial** in Egypt. They think it was created in about 1500 B.C.E. Historians now think that sundials were the first timepiece that divided time into intervals of the same length. Time was extremely important to Egyptian temple priests. Their religion had rituals that were performed at specific periods.

In the eighteenth century sailors at sea needed to know time to figure out their longitudinal location. No existing clock would work on the rolling sea. In 1714 the British government announced a contest for people to invent a clock that would work at sea. They offered a huge cash prize to whoever could solve the problem. In 1761 a carpenter named John Harrison developed a clock he called the H4, which was tested on a cross-Atlantic journey. It lost only 5.1 seconds. This exceeded the government's demands! But they wanted an astronomer to win the money, not a working class carpenter. After ten more years, Harrison finally received his reward. The H4 is now displayed in London's National Maritime Museum.

After the Sun had set each night, the priests would use a tool called a water clock to keep track of time during the night. Every evening, the priests would fill this vessel, or container, with water. Water dripped out of a small hole at the bottom at a steady rate. Marks on the inside of the vessel showed hours. As the water emptied, the marks became visible, showing how many hours had passed.

This Aztec calendar is actually two calendars in one. The solar calendar had 365 days. The symbols indicate the periods called *veintenas*, which are like our months. Every fifty-two years, the two calendars overlap.

Like these ancient cultures, our system of timekeeping is based on natural events. It makes sense that ancient people looked toward the skies to keep track of time, too. They may not have known why or how the skies moved, but they could tell that day and night and the seasons changed in cycles. Using only observations, they kept track of long-term time with surprising accuracy.

In 2000 B.C.E., the Babylonians, a very advanced ancient civilization, used a calendar with twelve months—each month being either twenty-nine or thirty days long. In the fourteenth century a civilization of people known as the Aztecs lived in Mexico. They are known for their scientific advances. In fact, their calendar varied between 260 and 365 days a year. Today we have technology to help us understand the mysteries of time and space. Yet, our calendar is still based on their system.

Space

You can use a ruler to measure an object's width and length, and height or depth. When you take these measurements, you are actually measuring the amount of space an object takes up.

Measurements are a precise science. It took thousands of years to come up with the methods we now use.

Euclid lived in ancient Greece around 300 B.C.E. In school, when you study geometry, you study his formulas. In geometry, a plane refers to any flat surface that has length and width. Euclidean geometry is used for flat surfaces. Cities and farms on flat land can be laid out using his theories.

One of Euclid's most famous methods of understanding space involved triangles. All triangles have three angles, whose measures total 180 degrees. An isosceles triangle, shown in the diagram, has two equal lengths. The bottom two angles are equal degrees.

These facts about triangles are the basis of a process of measurement called *triangulation*. Using triangulation, we can determine the distance to a particular point at the top of an imagined triangle by measuring the angles on either end of the baseline.

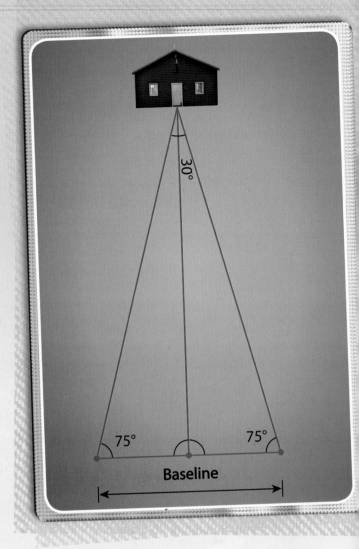

Surveyors can use triangulation to figure out how far a house is from a road. Using the house as the top point of the triangle, the surveyor puts out two poles to mark either end of the baseline. Once this triangle is established, the surveyor measures the angles at both ends of the baseline (75 degrees). From this, he can determine the size of the third angle (30 degrees). He can then use a formula to determine the length of a straight line up the center.

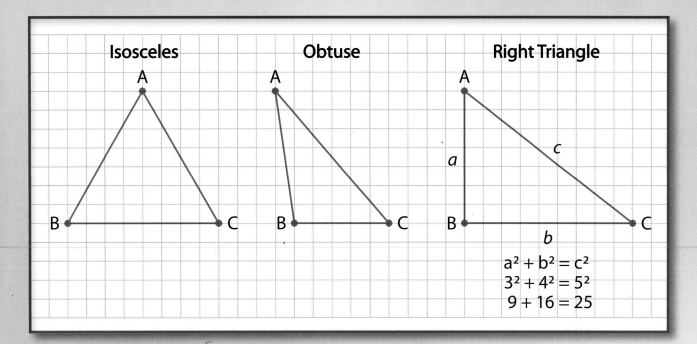

Isosceles

A

B   C

Obtuse

A

B   C

Right Triangle

A

a

c

B

b

C

$$a^2 + b^2 = c^2$$
$$3^2 + 4^2 = 5^2$$
$$9 + 16 = 25$$

Triangulation can also locate a star's distance from Earth, which appears flat, but actually is not. So, this method is not completely accurate for taking space measurements.

In about 6 B.C.E., Pythagoras used Euclid's ideas to find the shortest distance between two points. He drew a right triangle to connect the points—the longest side was called the hypotenuse. His formula was $a^2 + b^2 = c^2$. The two shorter sides, a and b, when squared, would always add up to the square of the longer side (c^2). The diagram above shows an example.

Yet, Euclid's theories have their limits, as they can only measure flat surfaces. In the world, there are very few totally flat surfaces. Earth is covered with hills and valleys. And, even more, Earth itself is not flat. What was needed was a new kind of formula, one that could be applied to any surface. Centuries later, this problem would be solved.

This graph shows the three types of triangles that Euclid determined. Pythagoras used a right triangle to find the shortest distance between two points.

Euclid's two-thousand-year-old ideas for triangulation are used for Global Positioning Systems (GPS) today. The angles of two satellites in space that are an equal distance from your location are measured, which means this location acts as the third angle of a triangle. Since all three angles add up to 180 degrees, a third satellite pinpoints your location.

In the nineteenth century a German mathematician named Bernhard Riemann realized that Euclidean geometry couldn't accurately measure every surface—it could not measure distances on Earth's surface. He realized that any curved surface needed a different kind of geometry. When a surface curves, distance grows longer. Think about it. A straight, flat road between two points is shorter than a road that goes up a hill and back down between those same two points. Since Earth is round, its surface must curve between any two points. Yet, that's not all Riemann figured out.

All objects that take up space have mass, which is the measure of how much matter is in an object. Riemann thought that mass curves space. He used complicated equations to prove it. His equations came in handy when relativity was being researched.

Riemann was a brilliant mathematician who formulated complicated equations to prove his physics theories. How complicated? The equation below is just part of one of them. Einstein was very interested in how Riemann's equations could be applied to objects in outer space.

Look at the photo of the trampoline. If the child were not standing on it, the surface would be flat across. For instance, suppose it measured 6 feet (2 meters) across with no one on it. Yet, the child has mass. The trampoline, which must stretch, curves under the added mass. If the surface of the trampoline were measured now, it would be longer than 6 feet (2 m)!

You already learned how motion and time could be relative to your frame of reference. Now let's see how space can be relative.

Black holes form when a dying star collapses in on itself. The result is a powerful mass that pulls in everything around it. It even pulls in space, which appears to bend into what looks like a deep . . . black hole! Scientists consider black holes one of the last frontiers left to explore.

$$F_x{}^2 + F_y{}^2 = (\Phi_\xi{}^2 + \Phi_\eta{}^2)(\phi_\xi{}^2 + \phi_y{}^2),$$
$$G_x{}^2 + G_y{}^2 = (\Gamma_\xi{}^2 + \Gamma_\eta{}^2)(\phi_x{}^2 + \phi_y{}^2),$$
$$F_x G_x + F_y G_y = (\Phi_\xi \Gamma_\xi + \Phi_\eta \Gamma_\eta)(\phi_x{}^2 + \phi_y{}^2);$$

The mass of the child standing on the trampoline makes the fabric curve beneath her. Einstein wondered if space were like that fabric: would it curve beneath the mass of large planets?

Light

When you look at an object, you think you are seeing it. Yet, all you're really seeing is light reflecting off molecules, or tiny particles. The words you see on this page are merely colors against a background. Also, without light, there would be no color. So light is all that our eyes can actually see.

There are many forms of energy. The electromagnetic spectrum is energy that travels in waves and spreads out, or radiates, as it travels. The diagram below shows the electromagnetic spectrum. Some of these names may sound familiar to you! X rays that are taken in a hospital use a form of electromagnetic radiation. Radio waves that you hear fall on the spectrum. Microwaves and cell phones all use forms of energy that are part of this spectrum.

Visible light is a form of electromagnetic energy. It is the only form that you can see. For years, scientists argued about whether light was made of particles or waves. Now we know light is unique. It acts like particles and a wave.

Most objects with mass naturally move in a straight line. If light was just particles, it would make sense to think that it traveled in a straight line. If it hit an object, light would either be absorbed (taken in), refracted (bent), or reflected (bounced back). When light is absorbed, we do not see it. We only see reflected and refracted light. Water refracts light. If you put a straw in a glass of water, the straw appears bent at the surface. It is as if the bottom and top don't connect. Yet, it is the light wave that has changed direction. A mirror reflects light. Many other objects reflect light, too.

Wavelength and frequency are two properties common to all forms of electromagnetic energy. Only visible light has a wavelength and frequency that our eyes can see.

The Electromagnetic Spectrum

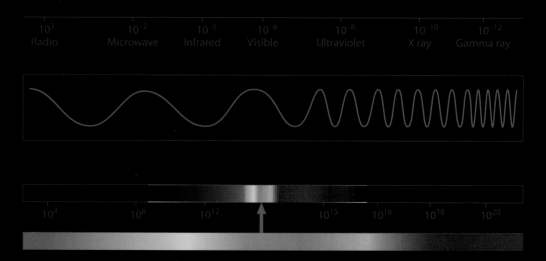

10^3	10^{-2}	10^{-5}	10^{-6}	10^{-8}	10^{-10}	10^{-12}
Radio	Microwave	Infrared	Visible	Ultraviolet	X ray	Gamma ray

| 10^4 | 10^8 | 10^{12} | 10^{15} | 10^{16} | 10^{18} | 10^{20} |

What we see as colors is actually just reflected light. Each color travels at a different wavelength. Objects absorb some wavelengths, and reflect others. An apple reflects longer wavelengths, and these appear red. Shorter wavelengths of light appear blue.

Light also moves as a wave that scatters and spreads. When an object absorbs light, some of the light is visible because it gets scattered. Light waves spread out from a light source.

A blue sky means a beautiful day. What makes our sky blue? Our atmosphere is made of gases and dust. As light travels through it, most of the longer wavelengths, which appear as red and yellow, travel straight through it. The shorter, blue wavelengths are absorbed by the molecules and reflected all around, making the sky appear blue.

White light is made of all the colors of visible light. Each color has a different wavelength. The wavelengths refract at different angles. When white light refracts through this prism, all the colors separate and become visible. The same thing happens when light passes through air and water molecules in the atmosphere, creating rainbows.

Some objects, like mirrors, reflect light, which allows us to see ourselves.

We now know that light travels in waves. These waves move up and down so quickly, that it only appears to travel in a straight line. The truth is that light takes the shortest, easiest route from one point to another.

Light also moves fast. Years ago it was thought that there was no speed limit to light. Galileo once attempted to measure its speed, but without proper technology, the experiment was a failure. In the 1670s a Danish astronomer named Ole Roemer observed one of Jupiter's moons, Io, orbiting the planet. Io circled Jupiter every 1.6 days, and Roemer should have been able to predict the exact location of it. Yet, when Jupiter was farther away from Earth, it appeared as though Io was behind schedule. Roemer finally figured out that this was because light had to travel farther to reach his eyes. Through his observations, Roemer determined that light travels at a speed of 186,000 miles per second (300,000 kilometers per second)! Modern technology, including spaceships with lasers and timers, proved that Roemer was close to exact.

On Earth, light slows down because it must travel through matter, like air and water. Yet, space is like a vacuum, or an area empty of matter, meaning there is nothing to slow down light in space. In fact, Einstein predicted that because of this, light would travel at a constant speed of 186,000 miles per second (300,000 km/s) in space. Again, he has been proven right.

Although light can't be slowed down in space, it can be bent. Is it by the mass of the planets? This could be true, but there's another force out there that was discovered by Isaac Newton.

Galileo's plan for measuring the speed of light was simple. He and an assistant stood a distance apart, and held lanterns that could be covered. One would uncover his lantern, and the other would measure how long it took the light to reach him. They would then divide this by the distance. The method was unsuccessful. Of light's speed, Galileo noted that, if not instantaneous, it is extremely rapid. He also noted that light moved at least ten times faster than sound. Also interesting? He most likely used a water clock such as those used by ancient Egyptian priests.

This flashlight shows one of light's wave properties. As it moves, it spreads out. If light were made up only of particles, the beam from this flashlight would not spread from the source. It would move straight out in a round shape and size that match the bulb.

Newtonian Physics

Legend has it that in 1666, a physicist named Sir Isaac Newton was resting under an apple tree when he was rudely awakened by an apple crashing down on his head. He began to wonder. Why does an apple fall down, and not up?

Newton's theories were based on three absolutes, or unchanging concepts. He felt that time was the same all over the universe; that an object took up the same amount of space, no matter where it was; and that the mass of an object never changed. All of his theories are based on these unchanging absolutes.

Scientists had explained for a long time that objects were heavy, or had mass. Newton believed that gravity is a force of attraction between objects with mass. Newton theorized that gravity depends on mass and distance. Mass measures how much matter an object contains. Remember, any object that takes up space has mass. Less massive objects have weak gravity. Gravity around a more massive object is strong. Earth is more massive than an apple. The apple doesn't fall, but it is pulled down. Gravity is also the reason you don't float off into the atmosphere. Earth's gravity pulls you down toward its center. Contact forces push back up against your mass where your feet touch the ground.

Until Einstein, Newtonian physics were the most modern theories we had about motion. Newton described the universe as mechanical because he believed it ran in an orderly fashion, and only in one direction.

Gravity cannot be felt. It is a noncontact force. As gravity pulls you toward Earth, other forces push you back up. The chair of a roller coaster pushes against its rider. These contact forces can be felt. When a roller coaster starts to go downhill, the rider is lifted off the seat and feels weightless. The feeling results because for a moment, gravity is the only force acting on your body.

Gravity also depends on distance. The closer two objects are, the stronger the force of gravity will be between them. Weight measures the force of gravity on an object with mass. For our purposes, it can be said that a scale measures weight. Suppose a person weighed himself on the beach, and weighed 100 pounds (45 kilograms). If he carried the scale up a mountain, he would weigh less than that. Why? Because he is farther away from the center of the Earth. These beliefs made sense and worked mathematically. They were the basis for Newtonian physics.

Finally, there were some reasons why objects on Earth move the way they do. But Newton wasn't finished. He was going to apply his mathematical formulas to objects in space.

Newton wasn't only interested in motion. Like Galileo and Einstein, he wanted answers to questions about all sorts of energy. In fact, Newton determined that a rainbow was actually made when white light separated into all the colors of the spectrum.

Newton thought that the Sun must also exert gravity on the planets. He explained that its gravity is why planets orbit, or circle around, the Sun. Of course, this led to yet another question: why aren't the planets pulled right into the Sun? Newton discovered that gravity is not acting alone.

Newton wrote three laws to describe the motion of objects on Earth and in space. The first, often called the law of inertia, is the one most important to understanding relativity. *Inertia* is the tendency of objects to resist changes in motion. The law of inertia states that objects at rest want to remain at rest, and moving objects want to remain moving. In addition, a moving object will only stop if a force acts on it. For example, look at the first picture at the bottom of this page. When you roll a ball, it stops eventually. You can't see it, but a force called friction is working to stop the ball. Friction is the force of two surfaces rubbing together.

The second law states that the speed at which an object moves depends on two things: the strength of the force that acted on it, and the mass of the object. The force in this case is gravity, and it grows stronger as the object moves closer to Earth's center. An object with a small mass that is acted upon by a great force will be the fastest.

The third law shows that for each action, there is an equal and opposite reaction. For example, if two balls bounce against each other, an equally strong force will push them away again.

The pull of gravity toward Earth is what keeps us from floating off into the atmosphere. If you throw a ball straight up, gravity will eventually pull it back down. So if its pull is so strong, how do astronauts in spaceships escape gravity to leave the atmosphere? They must have enough energy to resist the pull of gravity. In other words, they need to go really fast. **Escape velocity is the speed needed to escape a gravitational pull.** To escape Earth's pull, the spaceship must travel no slower than 25,000 miles per hour (40,234 km per hour)!

Newton's Three Laws of Motion

Newton's laws of motion explained motion on Earth and in space.

Law I   Law II   Law III

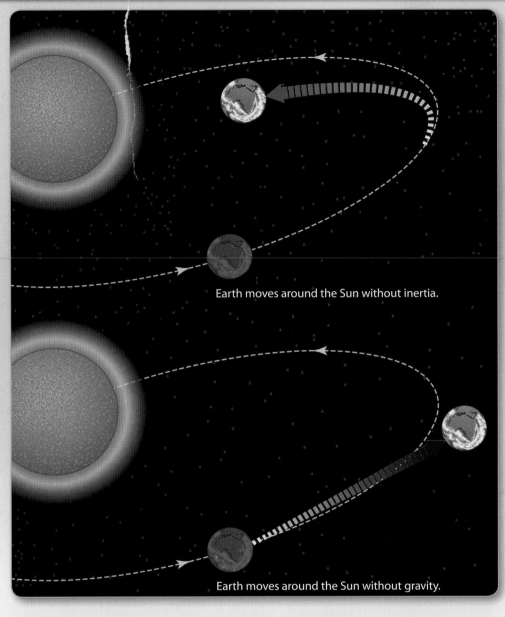

Earth moves around the Sun without inertia.

Earth moves around the Sun without gravity.

Without inertia, gravity would pull Earth and the other planets right into the Sun (red arrow). Without gravity, Earth would move forever in a straight line in space (blue arrow). The two forces keep Earth and the other planets in a path around the Sun.

Objects with more mass have more inertia. Think about what happens when you push a tennis ball, and a bowling ball. The bowling ball will not roll as far. It is resisting the change of motion because it has more mass, and more inertia.

The Sun is much more massive than any planet in our solar system. Gravity pulls the planets into the Sun. So why don't the planets fall into the Sun? Because of inertia. Together, inertia and gravity keep the planets in an orbit.

Moons do not orbit the Sun. They orbit much smaller planets. Remember, distance is a factor in gravitational pull. The Sun may be more massive than Earth, but gravity pulls the Moon toward Earth. The Moon is close enough to Earth to be pulled toward it, instead of the Sun.

Einstein Connects the Pieces

The Special Theory of Relativity

Albert Einstein questioned Newton's ideas of absolutes. His Special Theory of Relativity turned the world of physics on its head.

In 1905 Einstein was working as a clerk in an office. He hurried through his work so he could focus on his own ideas about time and space. These ideas turned into Einstein's **Special Theory of Relativity**. Basically, he felt that space, time, and mass were relative based on your frame of reference. His theory went against Newton's theory.

For example, Newton would have stated that if a car is traveling at 50 miles per hour (80 km/h), it is an absolute truth that the car is traveling at that speed. Einstein would have said it is traveling 50 miles per hour (80 km/h) relative to the still ground's frame of reference. Newton might say he got to work at 9 a.m. every day. Einstein would say that Newton got to work and the little hand on the clock struck nine at the same time every day. Yet, that didn't mean Newton got to work at 9 a.m. How can this be?

You may have heard of Albert Einstein and $E = mc^2$. Einstein thought he was anything but a genius. In fact, he often joked about how bad he was at math—his least favorite subject.

Let's start by going back to the speed of light—the only absolute, according to Einstein. An object trying to travel that fast would need an enormous amount of energy. Einstein believed that this extra energy would add mass. The mass would increase inertia. The object would resist speeding up, and never reach the speed of light.

According to Einstein's Special Theory of Relativity, as an object gains enough speed to reach the speed of light, it also gains mass. The excess mass will slow it down and prevent it from ever catching up to the speed of light.

Einstein thought that light was the universal speed limit. At speeds that high, Einstein believed that time, space, and mass would warp, or twist out of shape.

Einstein realized that mass was simply frozen energy. Einstein's famous formula is $E = mc^2$, which describes the amount of energy an object holds (E). You multiply the mass of an object at rest (m) by the speed of light squared (c^2). An object with a tiny mass could change into huge amounts of energy if it could move at high rates of speed. A single atom moving that quickly would have far more stored energy than a forest fire.

Einstein was known for being a poor student. He was expelled from one school. In fact, some think that Einstein may have had Asperger's Syndrome, a mild form of autism, which is a developmental disorder. People with Asperger's may find it hard to make friends or do well in school because they are incredibly intelligent. They find it hard to put aside their complex and interesting thoughts for subjects they consider uninteresting—like school, or small talk.

Einstein's theory proposed that the mass of an object could change due to its speed. How does this relate to time and space? Einstein believed that time and space could change: accelerate, or speed up, slow down, grow, and shrink.

Because the speed of light is constant, all speeds must be compared to the speed of light. His Special Theory of Relativity suggests that time is relative to the speed of an object's motion through space. This means that the next minute is not always a minute away. Suppose you were traveling at 99 percent of the speed of light. Einstein believed that at this speed, a minute would take longer. Yet, you won't notice. Only an observer moving at everyday speeds would notice. In fact, you would look at the observer and think that they were moving slower. Why? Because time is relative to your frame of reference.

Einstein combined this idea with Riemann's equations— that mass bends space. Mass can bend space and affect speed. Speed affects time, so time and space must be related. In fact, Einstein proposed that neither space nor time were absolute. They are one relative, changeable fabric called spacetime.

Einstein's Special Theory stated that something as small as an atom could release huge amounts of energy—if it moved fast enough. Einstein wasn't able to prove it, yet his theories were used to make weapons, such as the atomic bomb.

At the time Einstein was composing his relativity theory, many other scientists had their own, more complicated theories about physics. One such scientist, J. Robert Oppenheimer, went so far as to call Einstein "cuckoo" for thinking such wonders of the world could be explained so simply. However, Einstein was a big believer that the simplest explanation was usually the right one. He found this to be true in everyday situations, so he applied it to his scientific theories. Einstein had little proof to support his theories. This made them very unpopular with physicists of his day. Now, you'd have a hard time finding a scientist who didn't agree with Einstein!

Remember the example of the girl on a train, and the boy looking at the train as it passes by? Both think they are still, and that the other is moving. According to Einstein, the same principles hold true at incredibly high speeds: both would think time and space had not changed—and they would be right.

But what does this have to do with the speed of light? All Einstein's theories involve movements at superfast speeds. Think back to the train situation from the beginning of the book. If it's moving close to the speed of light, it would be a much better example of Einstein's theories. At speeds that high, space, mass, and even time can be very different for two observers. Time and space warping at normal speeds are barely noticeable compared to high-speed warping. At or near the speed of light, time, space, observer, and traveler are all warped in a way that cannot be ignored. As you are about to find out, things get even weirder at such high speeds!

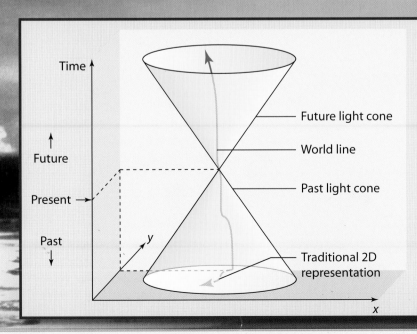

- Time
- Future
- Present
- Past
- Future light cone
- World line
- Past light cone
- Traditional 2D representation
- y
- x

Hermann Minkowski, Einstein's former math teacher, used Euclidean geometry in an attempt to prove that Einstein's spacetime theory existed. What was the problem? Euclidean geometry uses three dimensions—spacetime has four. This drawing may be helpful in understanding how space and time are relative to the position of an observer. Minkowski explained that all time and space are connected, but only inside the light cone—because nothing can move faster than the speed of light.

Special Thought Experiments and Proofs

Einstein was way ahead of his time. Because his theories involved such high speeds, there was no way to test them yet. So, Einstein conducted what he called thought experiments.

For our thought experiment, imagine a rocket that, on Earth, is 30 feet (9 m) long. It is now in space, traveling at about 90 percent of the speed of light. If we could measure the rocket in flight, we would find that it is now smaller—about 20 feet (6 m). Yet, if the pilot himself took a ruler and measured the rocket, he wouldn't see a difference. That's because he and his ruler also would have shrunk! The ruler would still show the ship to be 30 feet (9 m) long.

Crazy? Nope! Remember the basics. The rocket would be gaining mass as it sped up. As it gained mass, its center would have a stronger pull of gravity. At such high speed, the gravity would pull the rocket into itself—it would shrink.

A famous thought experiment is known as the twin paradox. Lets look at a set of twins who are both ten years old. One twin goes in a rocket that travels at 90 percent of the speed of light and the other stays on the ground.

From the frame of reference of the observer on the ground, the superfast rocket would appear smaller. Looking down from his rocket, the pilot would think the stationary rocket shrank. Who's right? You guessed it—they both are!

The traveling brother thinks he was gone for a year and a half, while his homebound brother thinks he was gone for forty years! When the pilot returns from his trip, he is just eleven and a half years old and his brother is fifty.

The slowing of measured time—relative to an observer's frame of reference—is known as time dilation. In 1971 an experiment showed that time dilation might exist. An atomic clock keeps incredibly precise track of time. One was placed on a spacecraft traveling around the world at 600 miles per hour (966 km/h). Another was left on the ground. The pilot returned with the on-board clock: it was slower by a few billionths of a second! You may think this doesn't prove anything, but 600 miles per hour (966 km/h) is only about .0002 percent of the speed of light. Remember that light travels at 186,000 miles per second (300,000 km/s). Compared to that, 600 miles per hour (966 km/h) is slow motion! At such a slow speed, the difference in time that the two clocks showed was not large. But, suppose that the spacecraft carrying the atomic clock was traveling close to the speed of light. The effects of time dilation would be much greater.

Atomic clocks work sort of like pendulum clocks, which move back and forth between seconds. Instead of a pendulum, the nucleus, or center, of an atom moves back and forth between electrons. Atomic clocks keep time more accurately than any other clock that exists. They even keep time better than Earth's movement in space. Atomic clocks are used to make sure the time is correct on computers, and to program the satellites that are used by GPSs.

Traveling near the speed of light would make individuals age and experience time differently.

The University of Utah has an instrument for detecting invisible rays in space. It's called Fly's Eye II. In 1991 it tracked a particle that we now call the Oh-My-God particle. That was the reaction of observers when they measured the amount of energy in the particle. It could be compared to a baseball that was thrown at 55 miles per hour (90 km/h)! It was traveling only slightly slower than the speed of light.

This is a view from inside a particle accelerator called the Large Hadron Collider. Scientists hope to learn several things by speeding up particles. They want to see if Einstein's theories can be proven. They also want to see if they can let the energy loose in a high-speed atom, without causing an explosion. Just how big is this accelerator? Compare it to the size of the man in the picture.

It's hard, if not impossible, to prove Einstein's Special Theory of Relativity. We do not have the technology to travel at 90 percent of the speed of light, and human beings don't have the ability to survive travel at that speed. Instead, we must rely on Einstein's own thought experiments to show us that his theory makes sense.

In 2007 a team of German physicists came closer than ever to proving time dilation. They used a machine called a particle accelerator to do so. This machine is just what it sounds like. Small particles, such as atoms, are placed inside it, and sped up.

For this experiment, two beams of atoms were sent through a circular track at high speeds. The scientists timed the beams inside the track using a precise instrument called a spectroscope that uses lasers. They used an atomic clock to keep time outside the ring. Sure enough, time had slowed down for the atoms.

The Large Hadron Collider (LHC) is another type of particle accelerator. Experiments involving the LHC will help us find out what happens when these high-speed particles crash together, or collide.

These particles will have a lot of mass and energy. They will travel through an enormous tunnel, speeding up as the journey goes on. Some worry that the release of so much energy could create a huge black hole, which would swallow Earth within hours. The scientists promise that only mini-black holes the size of an atom will be created. If their theories are correct, the black holes will evaporate, or disappear, immediately. Scientists hope to study the atoms and elements that are left behind. They want to learn more about what happens in space after an explosion.

This diagram shows the LHC. The close-up shot shows the inside of the tunnel through which atom beams travel. Behind it, the red line shows the circular path the tunnel takes across 17 miles (27 kilometers) of Earth. This distance gives the particles plenty of time to accelerate to 99 percent of the speed of light.

The General Theory of Relativity

Einstein's Special Theory of Relativity explained why things moved a certain way from within a frame of reference. What happens when the frame of reference is moving around a curve? Einstein's General Theory of Relativity answered that question.

Once you understand Einstein's Special Theory of Relativity, his **General Theory of Relativity** is easy. It extends the special theory to include moving frames of reference.

Euclid explained geometry for flat surfaces. Einstein's Special Theory of Relativity applied to nonmoving frames of reference. Riemann's theories covered geometry over a curved surface. So, Einstein's General Theory of Relativity covers relativity over curved space, too.

It begins with the Strong Equivalence Principle, which explains that all forms of matter accelerate at the same rate when pulled by gravity. Einstein believed that gravity's pull on an object is the same as its acceleration in the opposite direction. Since speed affects spacetime, gravity must, too. Riemann thought that mass changed the shape of a surface. Einstein took it one step further. He claimed that a massive body in space, such as a planet, would have a gravitational pull that changes spacetime.

A very massive object has strong gravity. In space, a massive object, such as a planet,

A strong understanding of math is not necessary to grasp Einstein's theories. In fact, Einstein once told a group of students: "Do not worry about your difficulties in mathematics. I assure you, mine are still greater."

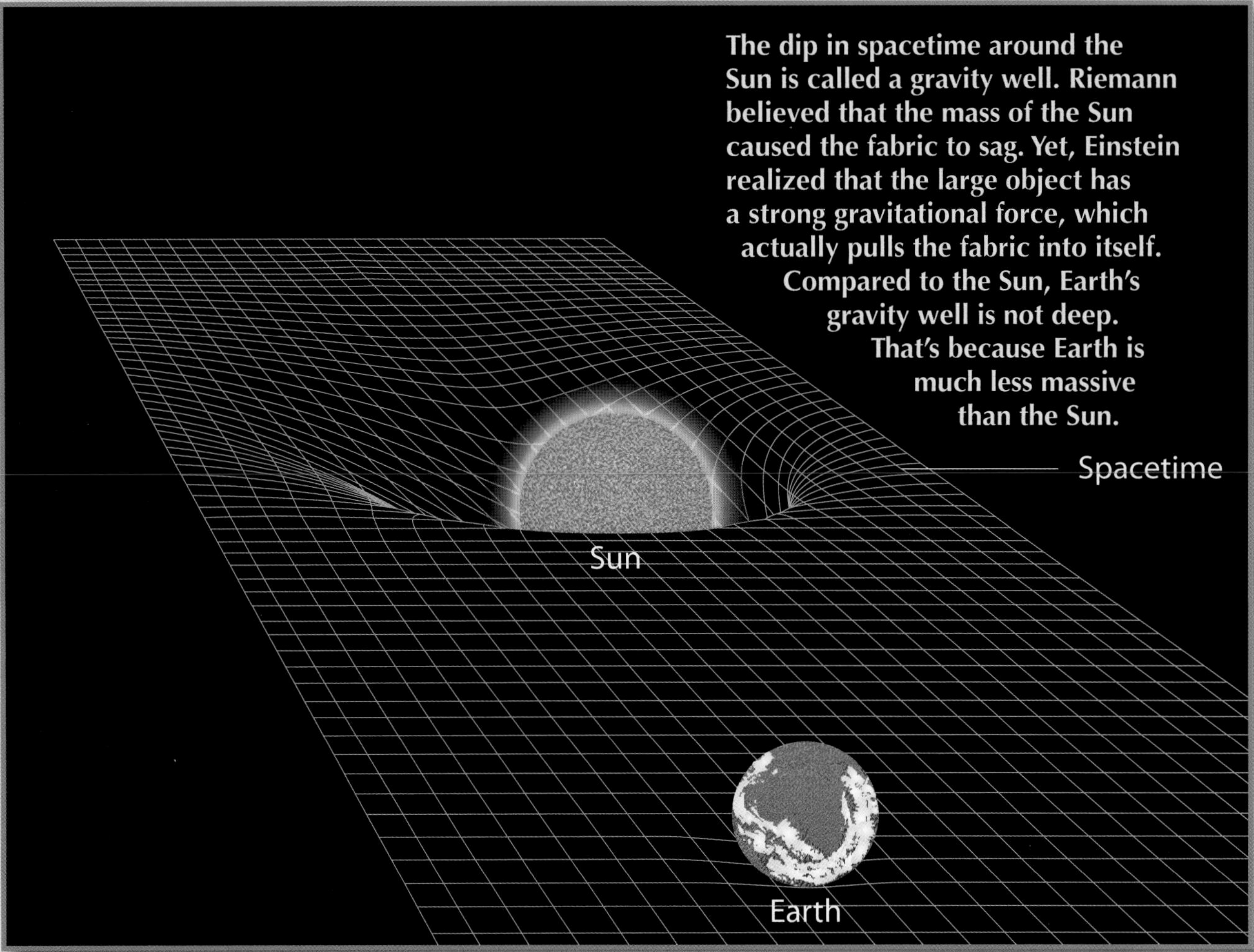

The dip in spacetime around the Sun is called a gravity well. Riemann believed that the mass of the Sun caused the fabric to sag. Yet, Einstein realized that the large object has a strong gravitational force, which actually pulls the fabric into itself. Compared to the Sun, Earth's gravity well is not deep. That's because Earth is much less massive than the Sun.

Spacetime

Sun

Earth

will pull on space—but not because its mass makes it sink. Rather, its gravity pulls on the fabric of spacetime, stretching it and drawing it around the planet, and causing the spacetime around it to twist out of shape. This warping is known as a gravity well.

Riemann pictured space as a giant rubber sheet. The diagram above is based on his findings, but applied to a grid. It shows the Sun, which is much more massive than the Earth, dipping in a gravity well. The grid represents both space and time. From the frame of reference of Earth, the Sun is lower in spacetime. Yet, from the frame of reference of the Moon, Earth would be in a gravity well. Both perspectives are correct.

Light is fast, but it is not instantaneous, or occurring without delay. When we see objects in space that are distant, we are actually seeing them as they appeared in the past. Luckily, the Sun is not that far from Earth—relatively speaking. It only takes eight minutes for sunlight to reach Earth. The sunlight we see is eight minutes old. Neptune is the farthest planet from the Sun. Light takes over four hours to travel to Neptune from the Sun.

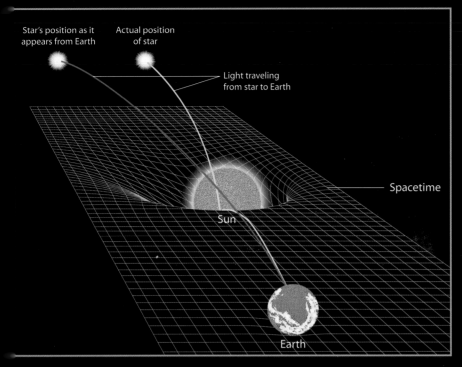

Star's position as it appears from Earth

Actual position of star

Light traveling from star to Earth

Spacetime

Sun

Earth

Light takes the easiest path. Like all other objects in space, it would dip into a gravity well. What is the result? From our frame of reference, distant objects appear to be in a different location than where they actually are.

Strong gravitational pull makes gravity wells. The same gravity will pull any nearby objects in space into a gravity well. Even light will be pulled in. That's because all waves move in the shortest, easiest path.

As light moves in waves, it spreads out. Some light will be out of reach of an object's gravitational pull. Some will be caught in its orbit for a while and then continue to move on. Much of it will flow down and back up a gravity well. This shift in light waves distorts the perception of an observer. The diagram above shows that from Earth, which is a curved, moving object, a distant star may appear to be to one side of a massive body. From a different frame of reference, the star may appear to be in a different location.

Astronomers are thrilled with this discovery. A gravitational lens forms when light from a very distant object is bent by a massive object. This effect allows astronomers to see galaxies that should be too far away to see with a telescope. Suppose a massive galaxy is between the Earth and a distant, less massive galaxy. That near galaxy will have a strong gravitational pull. The result? Light from the distant galaxy will be pulled toward its gravity well. Some light will appear curved as it orbits the closer galaxy's gravity well. Other light waves will take a shortcut through the gravity well, traveling through spacetime closer to us. You can see all of these effects in the diagram above.

It took Einstein ten years to complete his General Theory of Relativity. Most, of course, was based on thought experiments. It was considered his masterpiece.

Abell 2218 is a distant, massive galaxy. There are many galaxies behind it, too far to be visible even with the best technology. Luckily for us, Abell 2218 has a massive gravitational pull. Its pull creates a huge gravity well that pulls even light from far away. Do you see those streaks of light in the image? Each streak is actually a galaxy that is even farther away than Abell 2218. The light from these galaxies is pulled toward Abell 2218, and curves around its gravity well.

Where did the universe come from? The Big Bang Theory states that our universe is expanding all the time. The planets aren't moving, but space is moving them farther from one another. Imagine two dots on a balloon. As you blow it up, the dots get farther apart—but they haven't moved. An instrument called a spectroscope, which measures distance using light, confirms this theory. The spectroscope calculates the distance by measuring light waves—taking their bendable nature into account. The Big Bang Theory is based on Einstein's General Theory of Relativity.

General Thought Experiments and Proofs

Einstein came up with his relativity theories using just observations and situations he imagined. He used both to create "proofs" that his theories were true. Once technology improved, his theories came to life.

NATIONAL BUREAU OF STANDARDS

The United States has completed many unmanned moon missions. **Rovers** land on the Moon and examine its surface. During one landing, the strong equivalence theory was tested. Measurements were taken on the speed at which the Moon fell toward Earth. These were compared to measurements of the speed at which Earth falls toward the Sun. It turns out that both bodies fall at the same rate. Yet, Earth has a heavy iron core. The Moon does not. Even though Earth is much more massive than the Moon, both are pulled by gravity at the same speed. Earth, despite its mass, does not fall faster. This supports Einstein's General Theory of Relativity.

In 1976 an atomic clock was launched into space on a rocket. The rocket circled around the Earth once. The gravitational pull from Earth's center is stronger than the pull near Earth's orbit. According to Einstein's General Theory of Relativity, the clock on the rocket circling Earth would show that time had slowed down. Sure enough, it did. When the rocket landed, the clock was compared to that of an atomic clock left on Earth.

This is the first atomic clock, constructed in 1949. Today, some atomic clocks are smaller than a grain of rice!

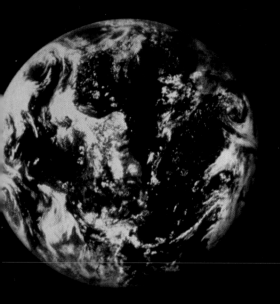

The clock that was left behind was slightly ahead, while the one that had been launched into space showed an earlier time. The difference was not huge.

The results are still limited by technology. So far it is not possible to send a shuttle carrying an atomic clock into orbit around the Sun. The Sun has a much stronger gravitational pull than Earth does, because the Sun is so massive. Suppose, though, that we could send a shuttle to orbit the Sun. Then we could compare the time on the atomic clock to the one that orbited Earth. According to Einstein, the atomic clock that orbited the Sun would be much farther ahead of the one that orbited Earth.

This photo of Earth was taken from the Moon during a lunar landing. Photos like these were taken for scientific purposes, such as studying our own planet's position in space.

Although Einstein is best known for his relativity theories, he had many other theories that helped us better understand science. One of these theories is still used to explain the nature of light. For centuries, the nature of light was debated: scientists argued about whether light was a wave, or was made of particles. Einstein was the first to assert that light has qualities of waves and particles. Einstein thought that the particles were packets of light called photons, which were made of energy. Once Einstein connected matter and energy in his special theory, the double nature of light finally made sense. Out of all the leaps in physics that Einstein made, he won a Nobel Prize for his work on the nature of light.

There is a reason Einstein couldn't test his General Theory of Relativity. It depended on huge, massive objects found only in space. Even today, we can only test his theories in space. Results have consistently supported his General Theory. So have natural occurrences.

Black holes are a naturally occurring phenomenon. They were not discovered during Einstein's life, yet, he predicted their nature. A black hole forms from a star that can no longer hold its mass against its own gravity. It collapses into itself constantly until it is the size of a pin. A black hole has more mass in less space than any other object. Its strong gravitational pull literally pulls a hole in spacetime. Einstein's General Theory of Relativity predicted that a huge amount of gravity would alter space.

You can't actually see a black hole. Yet, in this photo taken by a satellite telescope, you can see how gravity pulls material into it. Light enters its orbit and spins down to the hole before disappearing forever.

In order to escape from a body's gravitational pull, an object has to reach a speed known as escape velocity. Remember that to escape Earth's gravitational pull, an object must travel faster than 25,000 miles per hour (40,234 km/h). More massive bodies have higher escape velocities.

Could a body exist that is so massive, its escape velocity is faster than the speed of light? Scientists have found evidence to prove that a black hole is such a body. Of course, nothing really moves faster than the speed of light—not even light! A black hole's gravitational pull is so strong that not even light can escape from it. This is the reason black holes cannot be seen. It is also the reason they are called black holes.

Many of Einstein's theories were based on thought experiments and observations. Johannes Kepler was an astronomer who lived in the seventeenth century. He agreed with Copernicus that the Earth moved, rather than the Sun. Yet, he was obsessed with the belief that the motion of the planets followed geometrical rules. Although many of his theories were incorrect, he is still considered brilliant. He was the first scientist to insist that observations match theories. If they do not, the theory must be wrong. Einstein supported this method, which is still followed by all reputable scientists.

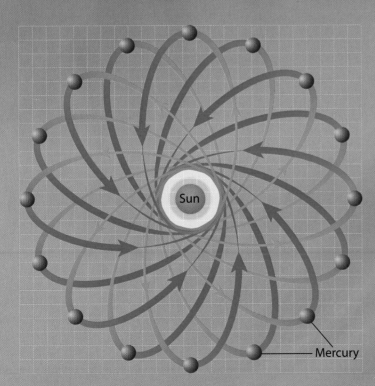

Another natural occurrence that supports Einstein's General Theory of Relativity is Mercury's orbit. Mercury is the closest planet to the Sun. As it orbits the Sun, Mercury wobbles up and down. The diagram to the left illustrates its strange path. One explanation involves the Sun's gravity. As the Sun rotates, it pulls sections of spacetime into it. Mercury is so close to the Sun that it is within the changing spacetime. This is because of the Sun's gravity.

This explanation is the best that physicists and astronomers have today. Einstein actually predicted Mercury's orbit would follow such a pattern, based on his General Theory of Relativity. Once technology had advanced enough, it should have been no surprise that Einstein's prediction proved accurate.

Mercury's orbit is unique because it wobbles up and down. Over time, its orbit looks like petals surrounding the center of a flower—the Sun.

What's Relativity Got to Do with It?

Einstein's theories of relativity are not just something to be studied. They should be put to good use.

Nuclear energy uses the energy trapped inside an atom's nucleus. Did you know that Einstein's relativity theories led to this discovery?

Nuclear power relies on the energy trapped inside tiny atoms. Einstein's Special Theory of Relativity explained that mass is equal to energy. When a tiny particle moves at high rates of speed approaching the universal speed limit, it gains mass, which is a form of energy.

A nucleus is at the center of an atom. We have figured out how to split atoms of certain elements, such as uranium. At a nuclear power plant, atoms of uranium are repeatedly hit with small particles traveling at very high speeds. If an atom absorbs one of these particles, its nucleus splits in half. Along with energy, more particles are released. These particles split more atoms and a chain reaction occurs. Nuclear power plants produce huge amounts of nuclear energy. This energy can then be changed into electrical energy.

Nuclear power plants use fewer natural resources than many other forms of energy. These plants are less expensive to run, and nuclear energy is less expensive to use for a consumer.

More than four hundred nuclear power plants are already in operation around the world, and dozens more are planned or under construction. This is because nuclear power does not use nonrenewable resources, or resources that are in limited supply on Earth. Traditional energy sources, such as electricity that is produced using coal, do depend on nonrenewable resources.

Studies of nuclear energy have also led to some of the best cancer treatments available. Radioactive material can kill cancer cells, track where cancer is growing, and even make treatments less painful.

Nuclear energy is not without its dark side, however. The waste products of nuclear energy are radioactive, and the chemicals are toxic. They can pollute water and land, making it unusable. The government regulates how they are disposed of. Nuclear energy is also used to make weapons of mass destruction, such as nuclear bombs. The blast of energy released is deadly. Radiation moves in waves, spreading poisons that could cause illness and contamination.

In 1986, a nuclear power plant in Chernobyl, Russia, overheated. Radioactive contaminants leaked into the air, water, and soil. Thousands of people died, became ill, or were disfigured. Governments now take precautions to make sure this kind of disaster doesn't occur again.

In 1945 the United States dropped nuclear bombs on the Japanese cities of Hiroshima and Nagasaki. Within days, over 200,000 people died. Years later, thousands of people—most of them civilians—were still dying from exposure to radiation poisoning. No other country has ever used such a devastating weapon. Yet, many countries, including the United States and Russia, have more than enough bombs saved to destroy the entire world.

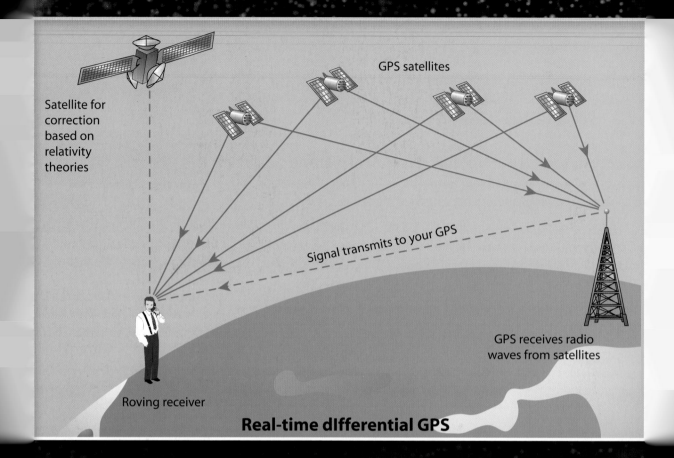

Each satellite in a GPS transmits the time to a GPS unit at the speed of light. The length of time it takes for the signal to reach the unit determines the GPS unit's location. The fourth satellite corrects for time dilation among the other three satellites.

Another practical use of Einstein's theories is the Global Positioning System (GPS). A GPS uses Euclidean triangulation to determine distance. It also uses atomic clocks. Most importantly, it considers relativity. The GPS network has twenty-four satellites that orbit Earth at a speed of up to 8,680 miles per hour (14,000 kilometers per hour).

From our frame of reference, the satellites are moving and we are not. The atomic clocks on board should move about 7 microseconds slower than our clocks do each day. This makes up for the effects of time dilation. Yet, the curve of spacetime in orbit is less than the curve on Earth. Earth's gravitational pull is not as strong there, so it doesn't bend spacetime as much. The clocks on the satellites should appear to move 45 microseconds faster than our clocks do. So, the clocks on the satellites are set to move forward 38 microseconds each day. If we did not take the effects of relativity into account, GPSs would soon become obsolete.

Knowledge gained from Einstein's theories may also help us understand how the universe began. Scientists use particle accelerators to figure out the best way to capture energy. New colliders have another purpose. They hope to recreate a small version of the Big Bang Theory, which explains the origins of our universe. In 1922 a Russian mathematician named Alexander Friedmann came up with a theory based on Einstein's General Theory of Relativity. It states that our universe was once a tiny, hot, dense speck that expanded over time—and that all the matter in the universe came from the energy in that speck ($E = mc^2$). Physicists hope particle accelerators can recreate that atmosphere. They want a better picture of what the universe looked like just moments after its birth.

The relativity theories answered many questions, as well as raised some new ones. Einstein predicted the nature of black holes. He also knew they made holes in the spacetime fabric. We don't know where those holes lead, but Einstein had a theory that could lead to another space and time. Is time travel possible? Einstein was right about many other possibilities. Perhaps the curious minds of the future can find out!

Einstein was a pacifist, meaning that he did not believe in war. Yet, during World War II, he discovered that the Nazis had enough uranium and good scientists to make nuclear weapons. He wrote to President Franklin Roosevelt and urged him to make his own weapons before the Nazis did. He even helped the U.S. Navy with weaponry design. Einstein later regretted his choice, and returned to being a pacifist.

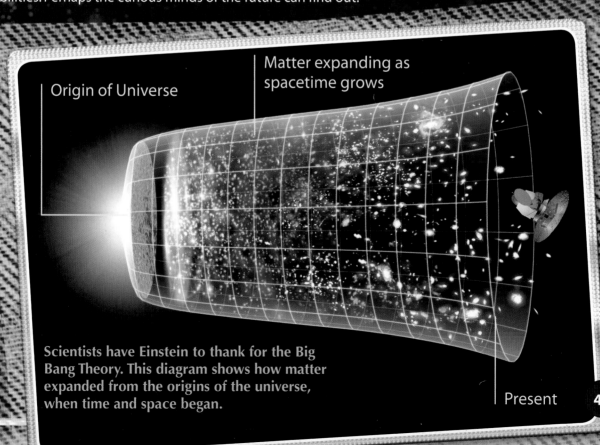

Origin of Universe

Matter expanding as spacetime grows

Scientists have Einstein to thank for the Big Bang Theory. This diagram shows how matter expanded from the origins of the universe, when time and space began.

Present

Glossary

body A mass of matter, such as a planet or the Moon.

escape velocity The speed an object must reach to escape a body's gravitational pull.

frequency A measure of how often a wave occurs within a given time.

General Theory of Relativity Einstein's theory, which states that gravity pulls all objects at the same speed, and that spacetime is changed by an object's gravity.

longitude Vertical lines that divide the Earth.

lunar Having to do with the Moon.

observatory A center for astronomical observations and studies.

pitch The quality of a tone that makes it sound high or deep.

rover A vehicle that explores the surface of an extraterrestrial body, such as the Moon or Mars.

space The region in which all matter exists.

Special Theory of Relativity Einstein's theory, which states that space and time are not absolute, and can change.

sundial An instrument for telling time by the Sun.

time zones Longitudinal divisions that keep a standard time.

wavelength The distance between the top of one wave and the next.

Find Out More

Books

Herbst, Judith. *Relativity*. Minneapolis, MN: Twenty-First Century Books, 2006. A comprehensive review of the Theory of Relativity aimed at readers at the junior high level and older.

Herweck, Don, and Kopecky, Michael E. *Albert Einstein and His Theory of Relativity*. Bloomington, MN: Compass Point Books, 2009. A biography of Albert Einstein and a description of the Theory of Relativity.

Russell, P. M. *The Wormhole Adventures: Time Is Relative*. Frederick, MD: PublishAmerica, 2007. A fictionalized account of time travel through a wormhole in space. As the characters travel through time, the theories involved are explained in clear language and through useful examples.

Websites

http://science.howstuffworks.com/relativity.htm
This website explains the details of Einstein's Special Theory of Relativity,

Index

Aristotle, 7
astronomy, 5, 8–10
atomic bomb, 28
atomic clock, 31, 33, 38–39, 44

Babylonian, 13
Big Bang Theory, 37, 45
black hole, 16, 33, 40–41, 45

Copernicus, Nicolaus, 7–9, 41

Doppler Effect, 5

$E = mc^2$, 26–27, 45
Earth, 6–12, 15–16, 20–25, 31, 35–36,
   38–39,
electromagnetic spectrum, 18
Einstein, Albert, 5, 16–17, 21, 23, 26–30,
   34–36, 38–41, 45
energy, 5, 18, 23, 26, 28, 32–33, 39,
   42–43, 45
Euclid, 14–15, 34

Fleming, Sir Sanford, 11
frame of reference, 5, 16, 26, 28,
   30–31, 34–36, 44
frequency, 5, 18

Galilei, Galileo, 8–9, 20–21, 23
General Theory of Relativity, 34, 37, 40–41
geocentric, 6
gravity, 22–25, 30, 34–36, 38, 40–41, 44
gravity well, 35–36

Harrison, John, 12
heliocentric, 8

inertia, 24–26

Large Hadron Collider (LHC), 32, 33
longitude, 10–11

mass, 11, 16–18, 21–30, 33–35, 40, 42–43
Minkowski, Hermann, 29
moon, 6, 8, 20, 25, 35, 38–39
motion, 5, 6, 8, 16, 22, 24–25, 28, 31, 41

Newton, Sir Isaac, 21–24, 26
Newton's Three Laws of Motion, 24
nuclear power, 42–43

Prime Meridian, 11
Ptolemy, 6, 9
Pythagoras, 15

Riemann, Bernhard, 15–16, 28, 34–35
relativity, 5, 16, 24, 26, 29–30, 32,
   34, 39, 42, 44–45

spacetime, 28–29, 34–37, 40–41, 44–45
Special Theory of Relativity, 26–28
speed of light, 21, 26–33, 41, 44
Strong Equivalence Principle, 34
Sun, 6–8, 11, 13, 24–25, 35, 38–39, 41

triangulation, 14–15, 44
twin Paradox, 30–31

wavelength, 5, 18–19